INTRODUCTION

The dawn of a new liberality came in 1960 when 'Lady Chatterley's Lover' could be published. Then in 1968 the abolition of stage censorship allowed the rock musical 'Hair' to be performed - it summed up the values of the hippie movement: sexual freedom, drug-taking and rebellion against authority, especially against the Vietnam War. Other freedoms were found with the contraceptive pill and, at the end of the decade, easier divorce laws.

Among the headlines were; the scandal of the Profumo affair (1963), which involved the model Christine Keeler; the tensions of the Cold War (the Berlin Wall from 1961 and the Cuban missile crisis of 1962); the public fascination with the Great Train Robbery in 1963 and subsequent search for Ronald Biggs. In 1966 the Aberfan disaster struck when a coal tip tore through a school ("death's dark vale"). In 1965 Winston Churchill died peacefully, but it was the shock of the Kennedy assassination in 1963 that remained as a landmark in most people's memory.

Henry Cooper became much admired after two legendary fights with Cassius Clay (1963 and 1966); but Bobby Moore's England team were even greater heroes when they won the World Cup in 1966. The Sun newspaper replaced the Daily Herald in 1964, the first Blue Peter (1964) annual arrived for its five million viewers; in 1962 The Sunday Times colour supplement appeared with Jean Shrimpton on the cover, photographed by David Bailey.

Much of the driving force of the Swinging Sixties came from the synergy between pop music, television and fashion. Each impulse stimulated another - Beatlemania, Ready Steady Go!, the fashion of Mary Quant and Biba, the haircut of Vidal Sassoon, the Mods on their scooters, through to flower power, psychedelia and the cropped hair of the skinheads (at the end of the Sixties) that contrasted so dramatically with the hippies' long flowing hairstyle.

Tableware for all tastes, much featured in the glossy magazines like House & Garden. New styles emerged – Swedish design, for instance, was much in vogue. Whitefriars glassware produced a range of moulded vases in 1967
4   created by Geoffrey Baxter: (opposite top r. to l.) bark texture, the 'coffin' and 'drunken bricklayer' (tangerine in 1969).

Page						
4·5 Ceramics	14·15 Cigarettes	26·27 Private Eye & Oz	38·39 Radios - Coronation St.	50·51 Comics
6·7 House and home	16·17 Household	28·29 Teenage magazines	40·41 TV & Radio Times	52·53 Toys & games
8·9 Groceries	18·19 Cosmetics & toothpaste	30·31 Pop scene	42·43 Film posters	54·55 TV toys
10·11 Sweets	20·21 Fashion magazines	32·33 Pop music	44·45 James Bond	56·57 Gerry Anderson
12·13 Lollies & sweet cigs.	22·23 Fashion dolls	34·35 Beatles	46·47 Motoring	58·59 Space toys
	24·25 Magazines	36·37 Pop music	48·49 Holidays	60·61 Chronology-World

CONTENTS

Aspirations of the Sixties included the latest record player, eight track cassette player and colour television set — the Forsyte Saga became BB2's colourful drama of 1967. For hip, cool or with-it teens and twenties, the latest gear could be found in London boutique clothes shops. Above: Robert wears a suit from Carnaby Street's Take Six and shoes made from pig skin while Laura's black & white PVC mini dress has matching shoes. The decade of the small wheel, for mini cars and also the bicycle the Moulton cycle was launched in 1963 with 16 inch wheels, the Raleigh Small Wheel cycle (RSW16), above, in 1965 along with the folding 'Compa'

In 1967 Hornsea produced the popular Heirloom range - storage jars and spice pots (centre) were especially favoured. Portmeirion Pottery began in 1960 with design by Susan William-Ellis. Her cylinder coffee pot with elegant spout appeared in 1963 with the Totem amber-brown range (above right), Jupiter (blue) in '64 and the Eastern-influenced Magic City in '66. 5

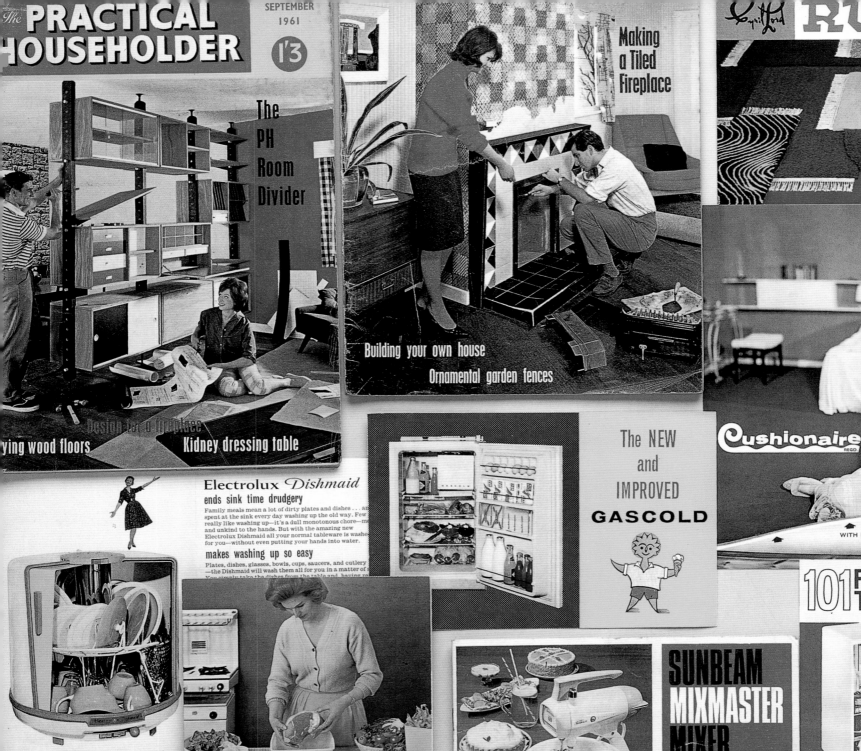

PRACTICAL HOUSEHOLDER

SEPTEMBER 1961

1'3

The PH Room Divider

Making a Tiled Fireplace

Building your own house
Ornamental garden fences

RUGS

Cushionaire

WITH FOAM RUBBER BUILT INTO

Design for a fireplace
Laying wood floors
Kidney dressing table

Electrolux *Dishmaid*
ends sink time drudgery

Family meals mean a lot of dirty plates and dishes... an spent at the sink every day washing up the old way. Few really like washing up—it's a dull monotonous chore—me and unkind to the hands. But with the amazing new Electrolux Dishmaid all your normal tableware is washed for you—without even putting your hands into water.

makes washing up so easy

Plates, dishes, glasses, bowls, cups, saucers, and cutlery —the Dishmaid will wash them all for you in a matter of

The NEW and IMPROVED **GASCOLD**

SEAL-AND-SAVE WITH **EON**WARE

101 **FRIGIDAIRE** TO BE WON

LATE 1961 MF46 4.6 cu. ft.

JUST BUY TWO PACKS OF ANY KRAFT MARGARI

SUNBEAM MIXMASTER MIXER

TRICITY REALM	TRICITY VOGUE
A capacious cabinet, but taking little floor space—all the features of a luxury fridge. Frozen food storage, 12 lb. for a month.	Height 44½ in. Width 19½ in. Depth 20½ in. Shelf Area 10.7 sq. ft. Capacity 5.4 cu. ft.	Sleekly styled fridge with all the Tricity features including ample door space for eggs, bottles and dairy food. Non-slam magnetic door seal and adjustable shelves, optional table top extra.	Height 36½ in. (with optional table top) Width 19½ in. Depth 20½ in. Shelf Area 8.4 sq. ft. Capacity 4.3 cu. ft.

You can modernise your home this week

...through the exciting new...

MORPHY-RICHARDS
'Blue Chip'
HIRE PURCHASE SCHEME

The **PRACTICAL HOUSEHOLDER**

JULY 1961

1'3

Making a Garden Fountain and Waterfall

Re-styling an old flat

Building your own deep freeze
How to print your own fabrics

Spanish Style Garden Feat

EXTRA inside!
3 Pull-out Booklets in the YOU-CAN-MAKE-IT-SERIES
● WOODWORKING
● FIXTURES AND FITTINGS
● CONCRETING

Modernising halls and staircase
Workbench and tool cabinet

In the kitchen, the latest labour-saving device was the dishwasher, much used as a competition prize. Cyril Lord carpet was the name for wall-to-wall comfort, "100% mothproof and fade resistant". 'Pass through' room dividers gave a new feel for space, and DIY extended into the garden where a water feature became the focus. However, continental travel inspired the use of patios for meals out of doors — or just for a quiet siesta.

In the new self-service supermarkets pack design became more vibrant to attract shoppers, and photographic images were no increasingly used on frozen foods and cake boxes. New brands included Coco Pops (1960), Heinz Spagetti Hoops (1966) and Mr Kipl Cakes (1967) - the box featured its own pop-up handle. With the popularity of instant coffee - most stores had their own Label - there was a trend for convenience; Marvel instant milk came in 1964, Angel Delight in 1967, Smash instant

8. potato in 1968, spreadable margarine in 1969 and another attempt to make instant tea. Soft drink cans began to ha

g-pull' openers for instant access from 1967. Breakfast cereals for children were linked to the popular TV characters, wile Tate & Lyle sugar promoted the film Mary Poppins (1965) with the memorable ditty "a spoonful of sugar helps the edizine go down" and "supercalifragilisticexpialidocious". Continental travel helped sales of Vesta dishes that ptured the holiday cuisine with Spanish paella or Italian beef risotto. Low calorie and slimming products were now part the daily diet like Outline low fat margarine (1969). Yogurt became the latest fad when Ski "with real fruit" arrived in 1963.

BLACK MAGIC

Mackintosh's
Quality Street
7¼OZ.(216g) NET   ¼LB. INC WRAPS
CHOCOLATES & TOFFEES

cabanas

CLARNICO **Real Fruit Jellies**
HALF POUND NET

mint chocs   LIFT   mint chocs

Dairy Box
Dairy Box

Dairy Box
QUARTER POUND NET

"Air-Sea-Land" BRAND
Glucose
BARLEY SUGAR FRUITS
FOR MOTOR SICKNESS AND FATIGUE

TERRY'S YORK
CHOCOLATE PEPPERMINT CREAMS
½ lb NET

CADBURYS **Milk Tray**
HALF POUND NET

TERRY'S YORK
ASSORTED CHOCOLATE
Neapolitans

Cadbury's ROSES CHOCOLATES
1 lb. PACKING WRAPPINGS
7¼ OZ. NET

14 27 9
52 * 17
Cadbury's Lucky Numbers
* 5 10 12

AFTER EIGHT
DESSERT CHOCOLATE

ROWNTREES **Today**
10 DIFFERENT CENTRES
HALF POUND NET.
GE' NEW MILK AND PLAIN CHOCOLATES

GEORGE PAYNE & CO. LTD.
CROYDON ROAD, CROYDON, SURREY, ENGLAND

Paynes 6ᵈ **toff-etts**
coated in rich milk chocolate

AFTER EIGHT
CHOCOLATE ASSORTMENT
HALF POUND NET

Bassett's Jelly Babies
RECORD OFFER SAVE 7'8
QUARTER POUND NET

CLARNICO **Mint Creams**

NESTLÉS milk chocolate
milk chocolate CROQUETTES

AFTER EIGHT

Bassett's
LIQUORICE **Allsorts**
WIN A TRIP ROUND THE WORLD
QUARTER POUND NET.
FOR FULL DETAILS SEE BACK

AFTER EIGHT
WAFER THIN CHOCOLATE MINTS

GLUCOSE
MIXED FRUIT FLAVOURED TABLETS
4 OZ.
BY Smith Kendon

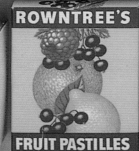
MELTIS
New Berry Fruits

ROWNTREE'S FRUIT PASTILLES

Matchmakers
ORANGE FLAVOURED CHOCOLATE STICKS

An increasing range of sweets offered such new tastes as Topic (1962), Toffee Crisp (1963), Aztec (1968), and from the makers of Mars bars came Twix and Marathon, both in 1967. Amongst many promotions was that by Cadburys in 1968 to award yourself a CDM, and in 1965 Michael Miles, host of TV's popular 'Take Your Pick' show, promoted the new assortment Lucky Numbers. Other new boxed brands included Matchmakers in 1968 and After Eight mints in 1962, launched alongside an After Eight assortment and dessert bar (but both lasted only a few years).

11

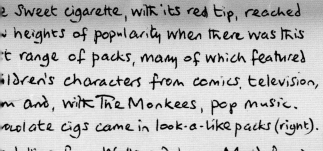

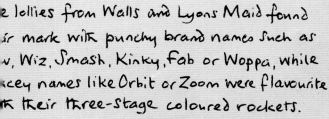

e Sweet cigarette, with its red tip, reached

heights of popularity when there was this

t range of packs, many of which featured

ildren's characters from comics, television,

m and, with The Monkees, pop music.

rolate cigs came in look-a-like packs (right).

e lollies from Walls and Lyons Maid found

ir mark with punchy brand names such as

v, Wiz, Smash, Kinky, Fab or Woppa, while

cey names like Orbit or Zoom were flavourite

th their three-stage coloured rockets.

TIPPED WOODBINES

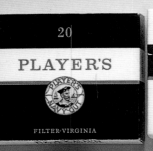 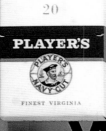  

10 FOR 1/4 - 20 FOR 2/8

 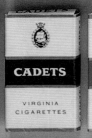         

During the 1960s smokers continued to switch from plain to tipped cigarettes; the 1962 Report on Smoking and Health gave added impetus to the swing to filter brands. By 1965 half of all cigarettes smoked were tipped, compared to just 15% in 1960. Heavy promotion of King size brands like Benson & Hedges Special Filter (launched 1962) and menthol brands like Consulate 'cool as a mountain stream' increased their shares, but in 1965 cigarette advertising on television was banned. The inclusion of gift coupons in new brands intensified competition; Embassy (1962), Players Nº6 (1965) and Sterling (1966) all issued gift books with an enticing array of 'free' items: a Dansette record player (5000 coupons), Jantzen Bri-Nylon swimsuit 'black only' (2200 vouchers), Moulton Stowaway bicycle (collapsible in 40 seconds) for 16,500 vouchers. Some brands like Guards (1959) and Nelson (1960) added coupons later to the packs. Some packs were upgraded to the crushproof flip-top variety. There were failures. Strand cigarettes were launched in 1960 with the slogan 'You're never alone with a Strand' — not many wanted to be associated with being lonely. Conquest was launched in 1968 but did not live up to its name and was withdrawn in the following year.

14

Plastic containers were now becoming part of the domestic scene, especially for the increasing range of washing-up liquids, for bleaches like Domestos, lavatory cleaners like Harpic and even, temporarily, for the scouring powders of Vim and Ajax. New brands included J Cloth (1967), Comfort (1967) Britain's first fabric softener, Ariel (1969) and for shoes "Self-shining polish". There were more aerosols (like Windolene spray), more soft toilet rolls, and a wider choice of pet foods.

nanufacturers increasingly relied on 'flash' offers that gave '4d off' or '6d off' the normal retail price, and washing powders
nquently gave free gifts – perhaps a plastic daffodil or tea caddy – with every purchase. Shoppers could now experience the
citement of collecting Green Shield Stamps and Pink Stamps (see page 1), an inducement to spend at certain retailers and
rol stations. Free gifts included a Morphy Richards pop-up toaster (8 full books) to a Lambretta scooter for just 155 books.

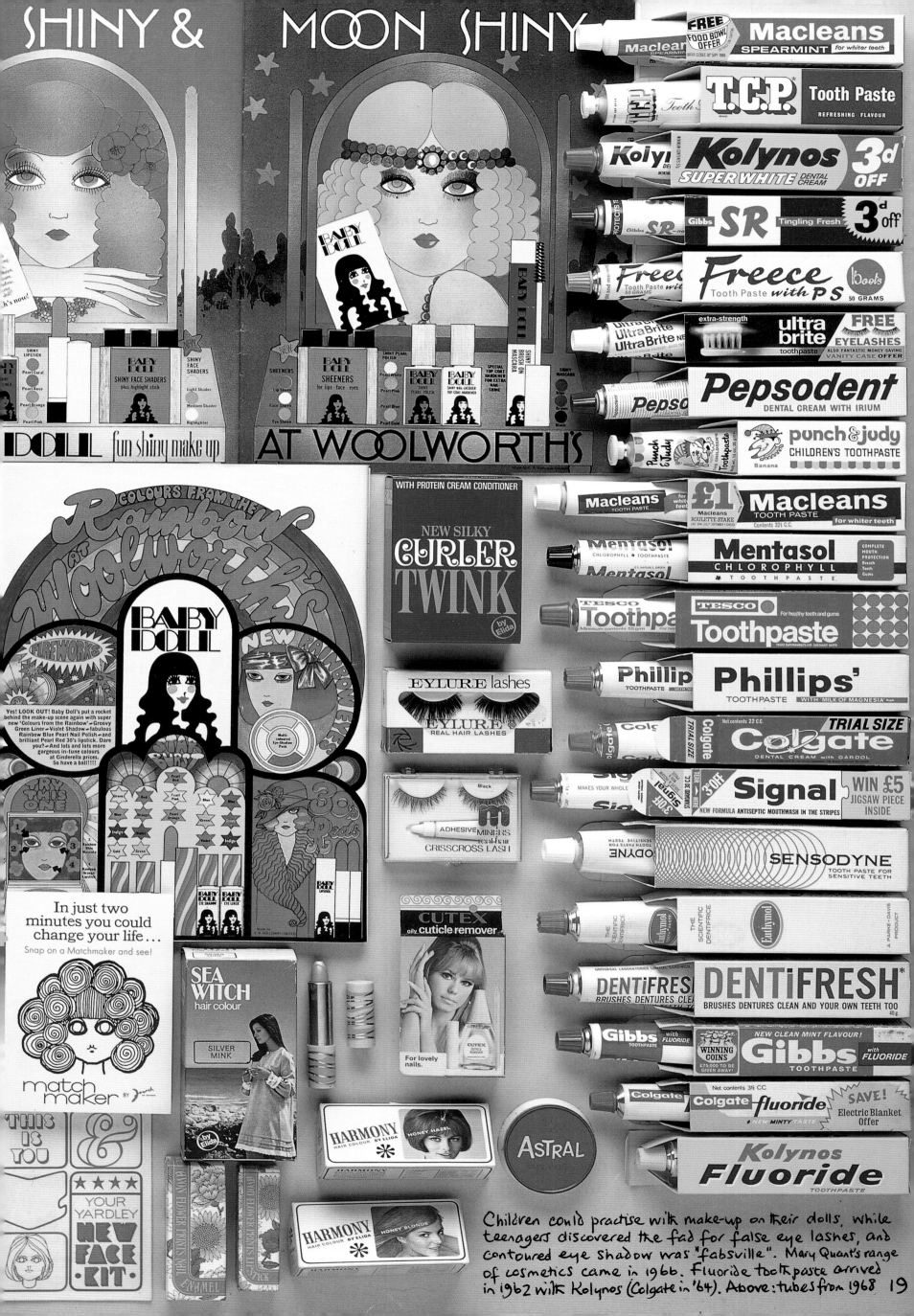

Children could practise with make-up on their dolls, while teenagers discovered the fad for false eye lashes, and contoured eye shadow was "fabsville". Mary Quant's range of cosmetics came in 1966. Fluoride toothpaste arrived in 1962 with Kolynos (Colgate in '64). Above: tubes from 1968

FLAIR

JULY 1962
1/6

A foolproof
holiday wardrobe

Lingerie—
pretty and practical

MARSHALL &
SNELGROVE

SPRING 1964

THE NEW YOUNG WOMAN
PETTICOAT
FREE COMPETITION WIN £100
and
A TRIP TO PARIS
Fashion
goes daring
after dark

Polly Peck

A selection
from our
Spring-Summer
Collection
1962

new city-status for the great
ttle indispensable summer dress
with the linen look in blended silk.
hoose from lollipop colours, add
white felt sombrero! No.573,
es 12-18 and short fittings
ps, a little more for size 20 and
ger.

MARSHALL &
...OVE

xclusiv

SPRING/SUMMER
1964

3
Pretty, shifty look with neckline etched
in contrast, the belt to tie as you please.
Peat, cavalry beige, french navy or black.
Sizes 36″—42″. 15 gns.

4
Timeless twinset, buttoned in gilt f
Jade, misty blue, mocha brow
hunting pink, silver sand or bla
Sizes 36″—42″. 13 gns.

WITH IT STYLES FOR THE MODERNS

Berkertex

Go Girl Go-Fabulous MODERN DRESSES

VOGUE
GREAT NEW LOOKS
WITH MORE THAN
A DASH OF FLATTERY

BEAUTY
THROUGH A
MAGNIFYING GLASS

WHAT'S NEW IN PRINT:
CASHMERE

ELIZABETH AND
RICHARD BURTON
OBSERVATIONS
BY A FAMOUS DIRECTOR

AUSTRALIA:
THE LUCKY COUNTRY

California
"The Look You Love"

During the Sixties, influences for fashion moved from haute
couture to the London boutiques like those of Biba, Bus
Stop and Mary Quant's Bazaar. It was the youth revolution
that now became the catalyst for change - new freedoms
gave rise to natural curves, trouser suits and mini skirts
(some dry cleaners charged 2d per inch). In the early Sixties,
model Jean Shrimpton inspired girls to grow long blonde hair;
from 1965 Twiggy became the boyish symbol of
swinging London, where Carnaby Street was the focus
for change in men's fashion, encouraged by the Mods.
Magazines increasingly focussed on fashion; just
out were Flair (1960), Petticoat (1966) and Fashion (1968).

20

The doll success of the Sixties was the teenage fashion doll. Mattel's Barbie doll had been launched in the USA during 1959, coming to Britain in 1961. Barbie's curvacious body and extensive range of fashionable outfits made her a favourite toy amongst girls. Ken, Barbie's boyfriend, also came over in 1961, followed by more friends and family: little sister Skipper (1964), best friend Midge (1963), Ken's buddy Allan (1964), Skipper's friends Ricky and Skooter (both 1965), Barbie's modern cousin Francie (1966) and British friend Stacey (1967). Greater mobility came in 1965 when bendable legs were introduced, then 'twist 'n turn' in 1967 and talking Barbie in 1969. A Twiggy doll arrived in 1967 with her own trendy outfit

22

Sindy was Britain's fashion doll, made by Pedigree and launched in 1963 - "Sindy is more than a doll, she's a real personality. The free, swinging, grown-up girl who lives her own life and dresses the way she likes". Sindy's boyfriend Paul, followed in 1965 - "the well-dressed young man whose clothes are designed for a free-wheeling life". Sindy's naughty little sister, Patch, arrived in 1966. Tressy came to Britain in 1964, made by Palitoy under licence from American Character Inc. The main feature of Tressy dolls was their ability to 'grow' hair, enabling children to match hi-fashion with hair style. Tressy's sister, Toots, followed in 1965 and then best friend Mary Make-Up, with wash-off cosmetics.   23

TODAY The New JOHN BULL

Week ending May 11, 1963

NEW PICTURE BINGO—£100 FREE

CHRISTINE KEELER AND THE WORLD OF DOCTOR WARD

page 3

the man behind America's 'Profumo scandal'

Tit-Bits

No. 4076. Week ending April 18, 1964

6^d Every Monday

Beyond the fringe!

The inside story of THE BEATLES by the man who had to get off their bandwagon

CARNIVAL

WOMAN and BEAUTY

NOVEMBER

GORGEOUS VELVET COCKTAIL DRESS CUT-OUT OFFER

WIN A FABULOUS PRIZE— GREAT FREE COMPETITION

PARTIES A LA MODE

NOVa MARCH 3s

A NEW KIND OF MAGAZINE FOR THE NEW KIND OF WOMAN

Mr Sofa the Psychiatrist

This is No. 1 of the British monthly with the 1965 approach. What's the isometric system? Mary Rand figures it out. What does Christopher Booker say about Miss C above.) Who's Mr. Blond? Pages & page Butterfield. Robert R

MARCH

ANN

Nº1 OF THE NE

SYLVIA SYMS – HEARTACHE AND HAPPINE
CALLAS – GOD GAVE ME A VOICE
TED MOULT – HIS OWN PAGE
CONTROVERSY – THE MARRIAGE VOWS
ROYAL FASHION – THE QUEEN'S WARDRO
EXCLUSIVE – MARY QUANT SWEATER
TRUE DRAMA – QUADS MOTHER'S OWN
GENEVIEVE DARIAUX – ELEGANCE FOR
GOOD FOOD – DICK VAN DYKE'S IDEAS
HUSBANDS – BY THE MET-MAN'S WIFE
CHAMPAGNE – 50 BOTTLES TO BE WON

SPECIAL FREE GIFT INSIDE

MODERN WOMAN

JUNE 1963 1s. 9d.

LIVING OUT OF DOORS: extra BEAUTY and HOME features

VOGU

SUMMER FOOD for picnics and parties

CAREERS guide for your teenager

FURNITURE for indoors and outdoors

PRETTY CLOTHES TO TRAVEL IN

1/-

JUNE 1965

Family Circle

INCORPORATING TRIO

LOOK AL
THE SHR
TRANSPORT
HOW TO C
YOUN
WORLD
FUNNY

Spot the famous faces: Ursula Andress (Vogue), Brigitte Bardot (Queen) and the new model sensation Twiggy (Woman's Mirror); in the news were Christine Keeler (Today) and Jane Fonda (Weekend). New magazines included Nova (1964) and Annabel (1966).

24

2/6
MARCH

WEEKEND
AND TODAY · SIXPENCE - No. 3281. JANUARY 10-16, 1968

COME OFF IT, JANE!

When Fonda talks of men and marriage, who does she think she's kidding?

— CENTRE PAGES

NADIA SANDERS
—this French actress is one of Dean Martin's 'Slay Girls' in the new Matt Helm

WIN A CAR

INCREDIBLE STORY

Queen

1 February 1968   Fortnightly 4s

WHAT IS THIS THING CALLED FOOTBALL?

COURRÈGES' FUTURE COLLECTION

BRITAIN'S OLYMPIC SKI-G and BB

TWO SHILLINGS

BELL
FOR THE YOUNG WIFE

wm
WOMAN'S MIRROR 11 FEBRUARY 1967 SEVENPENCE

The Brave Heart—story of a mother's courage

£2,500 to be won in a great new competition

Wonderful 8-page book
Gay young tops to knit

Exciting news of things in store

slimming
and family nutrition

THE 100 MEAL DIET
Complete 8-page slimming course inside

WHAT'S IT LIKE TO LOSE 3½ STONE IN 3½ MONTHS?

THE PERFECT MEAL
A nutritionist and a great chef give you the recipe

HOW THE FAMOUS STAY SLIM From LBJ to 'the Saint'

FOOD YOUR FAMILY NEEDS
Make an expert's choice with Dr. Alan Howard

THE DANGEROUS YEARS: 'Puppy Fat' by Professor W.J.H. Butterfield

OVERWEIGHT and the PILL

March–April
THREE SHILLING

ew from Woman   SPRING NUMBER   **2/6**

BRIDE AND HOME
tomorrow's happiest young marrieds

FEBRUARY 1967

SHE   2/-
MONTHLY

40 to b

WIN dre Co

Se

HERE'S HERMAN!

PUNCH 30 APRIL 1969
TWO SHILLINGS

THE BALDING GENER

Punch

HALL OF MIRRORS

Private Eye was first issued in 1961 - edited by Richard Ingrams and supported by Peter Cook. It quickly established a style of poking fun at political situations; by the end of the decade it was selling over 60,000 copies per issue. Oz magazine came to Britain from Australia, launching the first UK issue in Feb 1967. It owed much of its success to outrageous and radical content balanced with strong visual messages and the power of psychedelic artwork created by artists like Martin Sharp. The 'underground press' spawned many titles, from the International Times (1966) to a plethora of short-lived ones as here: Piccadilly Gazette (1962), Allotrope (1965). Left-wing publications floundered as young people dropped out of political action to adopt the "alternative life-style".

26

DATE

JEREMY SPENSER
full-colour
portrait
INSIDE

Jackie
for go-ahead teens

№ 1

ro
for yo

honey

THE NEW MAGAZINE FOR TEENS AND TWENTIES AUGUST 1/6

You asked us: When to neck and when not?

How do I land that job? Why is my make-up

a mess? —— in this issue the answers to your letters.

6 STAR
PORTFOLIO
Cliff Richard
Anthony Newley

FREE
TWIN HEART
RING

SUPER FULL COLOUR
PIN-UPS OF CLIFF,
ELVIS, BILLY FURY
and The BEATLES

PERFUME TIPS FOR A
MORE KISSABLE YOU

DREAMY PICTURE
LOVE STORIES

COLOUR PICTURES OF
OUTFITS TO MAKE
YOU PRETTY IN THE

Boyfriend
EVERY WEDNESDAY   WEEKENDING JANUARY 25th 1964 No. 240
7D

GLAMOUR
Mirabelle
and marty
6d ON SALE MONDAY
WEEK ENDING
23rd MARCH, 1963

Romantic
all-picture
love stories

ADAM
TALKS
TO
YOU!

MARTY
and SILVER STAR
Romantic Picture Love-Story Weekly
5D ON SALE
MONDAY
WEEK
ENDING
FEB. 11,
1961

Romance
Radio Luxembourg will
play YOUR favourite
love song for YOU

See Our
SPECIAL
OFFER

Romance
Gay, light-hearted
picture serial
"THE GINCHYTIME
GIRLS"
BEGINS
INSIDE

Romance
"Suddenly—it's LOVE"
SPECIAL
SERIES
ON
DATING
AND BOYS

THIS WEEK'S PIN-UP — JACK KELLY

No. 84—MAY 5, 1962.

CHERIE
5d
For Exciting Love Stories in Pictures

SPECIAL INSIDE
THE CHERIE BELLE SWEATER
An original Cherie Knitting Pattern
EXCLUSIVE FOR YOU
See Pages 14 and 15

HEAD OVER
HEELS

HEY! STEADY!

As she came down the bus stairs the stiletto
heel of Carol Brent's new shoes caught in the
step and—WHAM! She found herself falling
headlong against a total stranger . . . with
her arms wrapped round his neck!

INT

GIRL 11 November 1961

Girl 5d
11th NOVEMBER 1961
VOL. 10 No 45
Companion to EAGLE, SWIFT and ROBIN   EVERY WEDNESDAY

Read About Our
Wonderful 2-way
Pinafore Dress
on Page Seven

Jill of New Town (Page 3)

Prince of the Pampas (Page 10)

Lettice Leefe (Page 6)

Helen
Shapiro

THE MERSEYSIDE SPECIAL
YOUR LETTERS ANSWERED BY... THE BEATLES inside

© Fleetway Publications Ltd., 1964.   5th September, 1964.

Marilyn
6d
EVERY MONDAY

STU
JAMES
OF
THE
MOJOS
FEATURED
INSIDE

GOING BACK TO
YOUR OLD SCHOOL?
THAT'S CRAZY!

IT'LL BE FUN!
I'D LOVE TO SEE
HOW EVERYONE'S
TURNED OUT

NEVER LOOK BACK

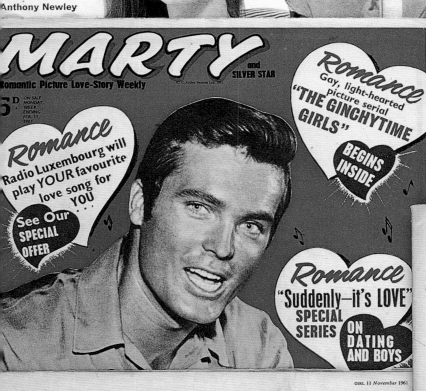
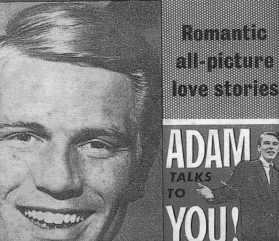

CUE ⁶ᵈ

BRITAIN'S FIRST TEENAGE NEWSPAPER

WEEK ENDING MARCH 2, 1968

POP STAR SHOUTS OBSCENITIES AT AUDIENCE

Big-mouth Proby does it in!

LIGHTNING LULU TOLD TAKE IT EASY

CUE TAKES OFF!

...cked a young ...h a few well- ...s making a come- ...udience, he lost his ...e give me any of ...he bawled at a youth ...with a party of girls. ...yone comes up on stage ...ys anything I'll knock ...on of him. I'll sue him ...of that!" ...drama had the audience ...field's New Cavendish ...aping. ...uth climbed on to the ...moved towards him. ● Turn to back page

WHOOSH! CUE takes off. So does Jimi Hendrix like a rocket — in this exclusive picture from his first film, 'Experience', being shot now.

UNIQUE! That's Hendrix, the man who plays guitar with his teeth and says each frizzy strand of his hair is a vibration.

Vol. 1. No. 1. Week-ending January 13th 1968 · EVERY FRIDAY

GO GIRL

Everything on the bright side of the scene **7d.**

those joyous original pop paintings to be won ENTER NOW!

FREE INSIDE! the Dangle 'n' Dazzle ear-rings It's the latest look!

SEE

NO. 1. OCTOBER, 1965

GRIPPING REAL-LIFE STORIES ROMANCE AND ADVENTURE

2/-

FORBI... L...

A 25 CENTS CANADA 50 CENTS U.S.A. 50 CENTS RHODESIA 2/9d. EAST AFRICA 2.50

SEPTEMBER 23, 1967. 1s. 6d.

Nº 1 GREAT FIRST ISSUE

FREE INSIDE INSTANT EYELINERS

THE BEATLES AT THEIR FRANKEST PAGE 6

WHAT'S WRONG WITH ALL THIS?

WHAT'S all the fuss about flower children? It seems that everyone over the age of thirty— particularly the national press, the police and the establishment generally—has had some- thing hard to say about the hippies. Loud cries of free love, junkies, nude parties. It seems any girl who throws off her office clothes on a Friday night and puts on a cut-down Indian bedspread is in danger of having herself labelled.

It means nothing to these critics that the vast majority of Britain's hippies are part- timers; weekend flower children with five day a week jobs. INTRO's countrywide investigation estimates that nine out of ten

FREE INSIDE *Valentine* **7d.**

PIN-UP **Brooch** of *The Herd*

AND EXCLUSIVE **Perfume** *Offer!*

Plus TWO BIG NEW SERIALS

FARE THEE WELL Sung by *The Herd*

EVERY MONDAY 27th April 1968

FEBRUARY 10, 1968 EVERY TUESDAY PRICE 6d

ROMEO
for romance

FREE INSIDE this luxury SHAMPOO and SET

OIL OF MINK SHAMPOO

SETTING LOTION

Specially prepared by eugene

IT'S SET-SATIONAL!

MARCH 2/6

19 IS NEW!

FASHIONABLE LOOKS FOR GIRLS WHO GO PLACES

WIN 19 DAYS AROUND THE WORLD!

WHERE HAVE ALL THE VIRGINS GONE?

FREE INSIDE! FANTASTIC MONEY-SAVING VOUCHERS

Plenty of choice in the growing teenage publications market. The magazine Date (1960) was short-lived, but Honey "for teens and twenties" made its mark from 1960 and Jackie "for go-ahead teens" from 1964. Aimed at the "young and fancy-free" (14-19 year olds), Petticoat arrived in 1966 (see back cover), and served as a shop window for mass-produced fashions— up-to-date clothes bought cheaply and discarded after a few months. Intro (1967) only lasted 6 months before being merged with Petticoat. In 1968 Go Girl was launched, quickly followed by '19' for 17 to 22 year-olds with a taste for sophisticated fashion. There was a strong following for romantic weeklies that relied on the heart-throb appeal of the new pop stars, - Marty, Marilyn, Cherie, Mirabelle, Valentine, Boyfriend and Romeo (most began in the 1950s).

BRITAIN!

'HAIR'
DISCOTHEQUE

SAMANTHA'S

3, New Burlington Street W·1

Soul Groups

Every Night

ST'
on-

DISCOTHEQUE

RECORD
4503

COPY OF
'IST'
ere

LA POUBELLE
CLUB FRANÇAIS...

16 Greek St. Soho. W.1.

LULUS OF KENSINGTON

INTERNATIONAL
DISCOTHEQUE!

LICENSED!

EIGHT TILL LATE!

La Première Discothèque Française
CARTE COMPLIMENTAIRE · FREIKARTE
Complimentario Billete
Bilipppo di Complinti

CHUBBY CHECKER
TWIST

THE TWIST!!
London W.1

COMPLIMENTARY

THE
PURPLE
PUSSYCAT

7 Finchley Road N.
ENTRANCE IN LITHOS R.
Telephone: SWI 2801 and SWI

MUSIC EVERY NIGHT

N A STRING

The British Entry by
Bill Martin &
Phil Coulter
For
The Eurovision
Song Contest 1967

RECORDED BY
SANDIE
SHAW
on Pye

3/-

NORTH OF ENGLAND EDITION

Sound

OP OF

HE POPS

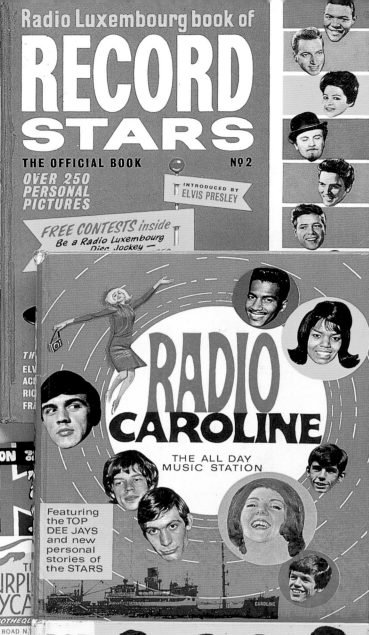

RADIO
CAROLINE

THE ALL DAY
MUSIC STATION

Featuring
the TOP
DEE JAYS
and new
personal
stories of
the STARS

CAROLINE

Radio Luxembourg book of
RECORD
STARS

THE OFFICIAL BOOK No 2

OVER 250
PERSONAL
PICTURES

INTRODUCED BY
Elvis Presley

FREE CONTESTS inside
Be a Radio Luxembourg
Disc Jockey

MUSICAL
EXPRESS

FANS SLA

Close-up on
SPENCER DAVIS
Sum-up on
CLIFF and SHADS
CILLA · LEN BARR
PINKERTONS

Plus top pop news

WORLD'S LARGEST CIRCULATION OF ANY MUSIC PAPER

EVERY FRIDAY PRICE 6d. FEB. 4, 1966 Registered at the G.P.O. as a Newspaper

Radio Times September 28, 1967
LONDON AND SOUTH-EAST

EIGHTPENCE

BBC-TV AND RADIO SEPT. 30–

Radio
Times

THIS
WEEK

RADIO
1
on 247

INTRODUCIN

The Swinging Ne
Radio Service

BBC TV Plans
for the Autumn

The Radio Times
Weekly
Magazine Featur
STAR STORIES
IN COLOUR
this week
SAMMY DAVIS Jnr
COOKERY
GARDENING

BRITAIN'S IN-TOUCH POP FASHION MONTHLY

DECEMBER

RAVE!

2/6

OUR CHRISTMAS PRESENT TO YO
Psychedelic Poster Insid
Fashion Exclusive on Wh
Christmas Cloth

POP
TEN

TEENBEAT
ANNUAL

Pop Round-up on Faces, Monkees, Move, Harum, Who and Scot

MIDLAND EDITION   No 431   JANUARY 31, 1964   6d   FEB 2 to FEB 8

TV TIMES

BRIAN
MATTHEW
introduces

THANK
YOUR
LUCKY
STARS
next Saturday 5.50 p.m.

JOE
BROWN
SUSAN MAUGHAN
KENNY BALL

The biggest dance craze of the Sixties was the
Twist, "the sensation of America" arriving in 1961 with
Chubby Checker. His follow-up, Let's Twist Again,
remained in the UK charts for 30 weeks during
1962. Other dances included the Bosa Nova and
the Locomotion. There were many opportunities
to promote records; Radio Luxembourg played
continuous pop music, but the pirate radio stations
from 1964 (like Radio Caroline and Radio London) took
a new audience until they were banned in 1967, the
year that Radio 1 was launched. On television, ITV's
Thank Your Lucky Stars was the focus on Saturdays
for pop talent, while on Fridays from 1963 it was
Ready Steady Go. Keith Fordyce hosted until Cathy
McGowan took over in 1965. After 175 episodes
it closed in Dec '66. BBC's Top of the Pops began
in 1964. Above: Vidal Sassoon hair cut on Rave! cover. 31

Todays **TOP TEN**

EMI RECORDS

1	WHERE DID OUR LOVE GO	THE SUPREMES SS 327	
2	I'M INTO SOMETHING GOOD	HERMAN'S HERMITS DB 7338	
3	I'M CRYING	THE ANIMALS DB 7354	
4	DO WAH DIDDY DIDDY	MANFRED MANN POP 1320	
5	WE'RE THROUGH	THE HOLLIES R 5178	
6	WALK AWAY	MATT MONRO R 5171	
7	HAPPINESS	KEN DODD DB 7325	
8	RHYTHM & GREENS	THE SHADOWS DB 7342	
9	A HARD DAY'S NIGHT	THE BEATLES R 5160	
10	IT'S GONNA BE ALL RIGHT	GERRY and the PACEMAKERS DB 7353	

E·M·I RECORDS LTD. (Controlled by Electric & Musical Industries Ltd.) · E·M·I HOUSE · 20 MANCHESTER SQUARE · LONDON · W.1

Ready FREDDIE go! with THE DREAMERS

SILLY GIRL · LITTLE BITTY PRETTY ONE
IN MY BABY'S ARMS · SHE BELONGS TO YOU

mono

3 CALL UP THE GROUPS (MEDLEY)

4 IT'S FOR Y...

5 I GET ARO...

6 ON THE ...

CATCH US IF

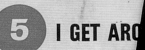

JOAN BAEZ sings SILVER DAGGER & other songs

fontana

TELSTAR
THE TORNADOS
POPEYE TWIST
LOVE AND FURY
JUNGLE FEVER

DIANE
PUT YOUR ARMS AROUND ME HO
YOU'LL NEVER WALK ALONE
MOMENTS TO REMEMBER
THE BAC...
Volume 2

A huge variety of music clamoured for top ten attention, from the new pop beat groups to country & western, soul, and novelty numbers like Rolf Harris's Jake the Peg (1966). Instrumentals came from the Shadows, Herb Alpert, and the Tornados with Telstar (1962), the sleeve showing the new communications satellite. Motown music (like Marvin Gaye) vied with the surfing sounds of the Beach Boys from 1962.

32

1	(3)	**HAVE I THE RIGHT ?** The Honeycombs Pye 7N 15664	**18**	(14)	**I FOUND OUT THE HARD WAY** The Four Pennies Philips BF 1349	**34**	(34) **HAPPINESS** Ken Dodd Columbia DB 7325
2	(1)	**DO WAH DIDDY DIDDY** Manfred Mann HMV POP 1320	**19**	(10)	**FROM A WINDOW** Billy J. Kramer Parlophone R 5156	**35**	(29) **THE GIRL FROM IPANEMA** Stan Getz/Joao Gilberto Verve VS 520
3	(4)	**I WON'T FORGET YOU** Jim Reeves R.C.A. Victor RCA 1400	**20**	(31)	**SUCH A NIGHT** Elvis Presley R.C.A. Victor RCA 1411	**36**	(33) **HOW CAN I TELL HER ?** The Fourmost Parlophone R 5157
4	(15)	**YOU'VE REALLY GOT ME** The Kinks Pye 7N 15673	**21**	(28)	**SHE'S NOT THERE** The Zombies Decca F 11940	**37**	(48) **TWELVE STEPS TO LOVE** Brian Poole & The Tremeloes Decca F 11951
5	(2)	**A HARD DAY'S NIGHT** The Beatles Parlophone R 5160	**22**	(23)	**YOU'LL NEVER GET TO HEAVEN** Dionne Warwick Pye 7N 25256	**38**	(32) **IT'S OVER** Roy Orbison London HLU 9882
6	(6)	**TOBACCO ROAD** The Nashville Teens Decca F 11930	**23**	(25)	**THE WEDDING** Julie Rogers Mercury MF 820	**39**	(50) **MOVE IT BABY** Simon Scott Parlophone R 5164
7	(8)	**I GET AROUND** The Beach Boys Capitol CL 15350	**24**	(17)	**WISHIN' AND HOPIN'** The Merseybeats Fontana TF 482	**40**	(—) **EVERYBODY LOVES SOMEBODY** Dean Martin Reprise R 20281
8	(13)	**IT'S FOR YOU** Cilla Black Parlophone R 5162	**25**	(40)	**I'M INTO SOMETHING GOOD** Herman's Hermits Columbia DB 7338	**41**	(30) **KISSIN' COUSINS** Elvis Presley R.C.A. Victor RCA 1404
9	(7)	**IT'S ALL OVER NOW** Rolling Stones Decca F 11934	**26**	(27)	**THE FERRIS WHEEL** The Everly Brothers Warner Bros WB 135	**42**	(35) **SOMEONE, SOMEONE** Brian Poole & The Tremeloes Decca F 11893
10	(5)	**CALL UP THE GROUPS** The Barron Knights Columbia DB 7317	**27**	(39)	**I SHOULD HAVE KNOWN BETTER** The Naturals Parlophone R 5165	**43**	(—) **THE BEST PART OF BREAKING UP** The Ronettes London HLU 9905
11	(21)	**I WOULDN'T TRADE YOU FOR THE WORLD** The Bachelors Decca F 11949	**28**	(18)	**SOME DAY WE'RE GONNA LOVE AGAIN** The Searchers Pye 7N 15670	**44**	(36) **RAMONA** The Bachelors Decca F 11910
12	(20)	**THE CRYING GAME** Dave Berry Decca F 11937	**29**	(—)	**RAG DOLL** The Four Seasons Philips BF 1347	**45**	(38) **HELLO DOLLY** Louis Armstrong London HLR 9878
13	(9)	**I JUST DON'T KNOW WHAT TO DO WITH MYSELF** Dusty Springfield Philips BF 1348	**30**	(22)	**THE HOUSE OF THE RISING SUN** The Animals Columbia DB 7301	**46**	(43) **(THEY CALL HER) LA BAMBA** The Crickets Liberty LIB 55696
14	(16)	**I LOVE YOU BECAUSE** Jim Reeves R.C.A. RCA 1385	**31**	(45)	**YOU NEVER CAN TELL** Chuck Berry Pye 7N 25257	**47**	(42) **SPANISH HARLEM** Sounds Incorporated Columbia DB 7321
15	(11)	**ON THE BEACH** Cliff Richard Columbia DB 7305	**32**	(26)	**THINKING OF YOU BABY** Dave Clark Five Columbia DB 7335	**48**	(—) **WHAT AM I TO YOU ?** Kenny Lynch HMV POP 1321
16	(19)	**AS TEARS GO BY** Marianne Faithfull Decca F 11923	**33**	(24)	**HOLD ME** P. J. Proby Decca F 11904	**49**	(37) **YOU'RE NO GOOD** The Swinging Blue Jeans HMV POP 1304
17	(12)	**IT'S ONLY MAKE BELIEVE** Billy Fury Decca F 11939				**50**	(44) **YOU'RE MY WORLD** Cilla Black Parlophone R 5133

PARLOPHONE

THE BEATLES

PLEASE
PLEASE

with Love Me Do

mono

Twist and Shout ★ The Beatles

all my
loving

the b

OPHONE

Twist and Shout

THE BEATLES

PARLOPHONE

THE
BEATLES
SCRAP BOOK

GEORGE HARRISON   PAUL McCARTNEY

RINGO STARR   JOHN LENNON

THE FABULOUS
BEATLES
JEWELLERY BROC

The Beatles

mono

PARLOPHONE

THE
BEATLES
LONG
TALL
SALLY

PARLOPHONE

PARLOPHONE

LOVE ME DO

THE BEATLES

THIS RECORD
MUST BE PLAYED
45
R.P.M

THE BEATLES   2'6

9d

WITH THE
Beatles

RINGO STARR

TALC
margo of mayfair

Managed by Brian Epstein, The Beatles were John Lennon, Paul McCartney, George Harrison and Ringo Starr. Turned down by Decca, the 'fab four' were signed by EMI on the Parlophone label. The first release was a Lennon/McCartney composition made under the direction of George Martin; 'Love Me Do' (above) reached No 17 in Dec 1962. The first of many number one hits was 'Please Please Me' in May '63; in the following year Beatlemania swept America. Their film A Hard Day's Night (1964) was followed by Help! (1965) and then the animated fantasy Yellow Submarine (1968). Sgt Pepper's Lonely Hearts Club Band was released in 1967, the same year as TV movie Magical Mystery Tour. Souvenirs galore: wallpaper, badges, nylons, talcum powder, bubble gum, scrapbooks, jigsaws, fabrics, record players... (see pl.).

PYX

WORLD'S POP STARS IN COLOUR COLOUR COLOUR

11th JULY 1964

Fabulous
ROLLING WITH THE STONES
& THEIR MATES GENE. P. HOLLIES BEATLES

Australia 1/6 · New Zealand 1/3 · South Africa 15 cents
Rhodesia 1/9 · East Africa 1.60 cents · West Africa 1/6
Sverige Skr. 1 · 25 inkl. oms. · Norge Kr. 1.50

THE WHO

Brunsw

CHENCELL
N-PROPAN

MY GENERATION

DECCA

y d pinkfloy

Columbia
EMI

ROLLING STONES   LET

mono L.K 4605

DECCA

OFE 8622

THE MOODY BLUES

STON

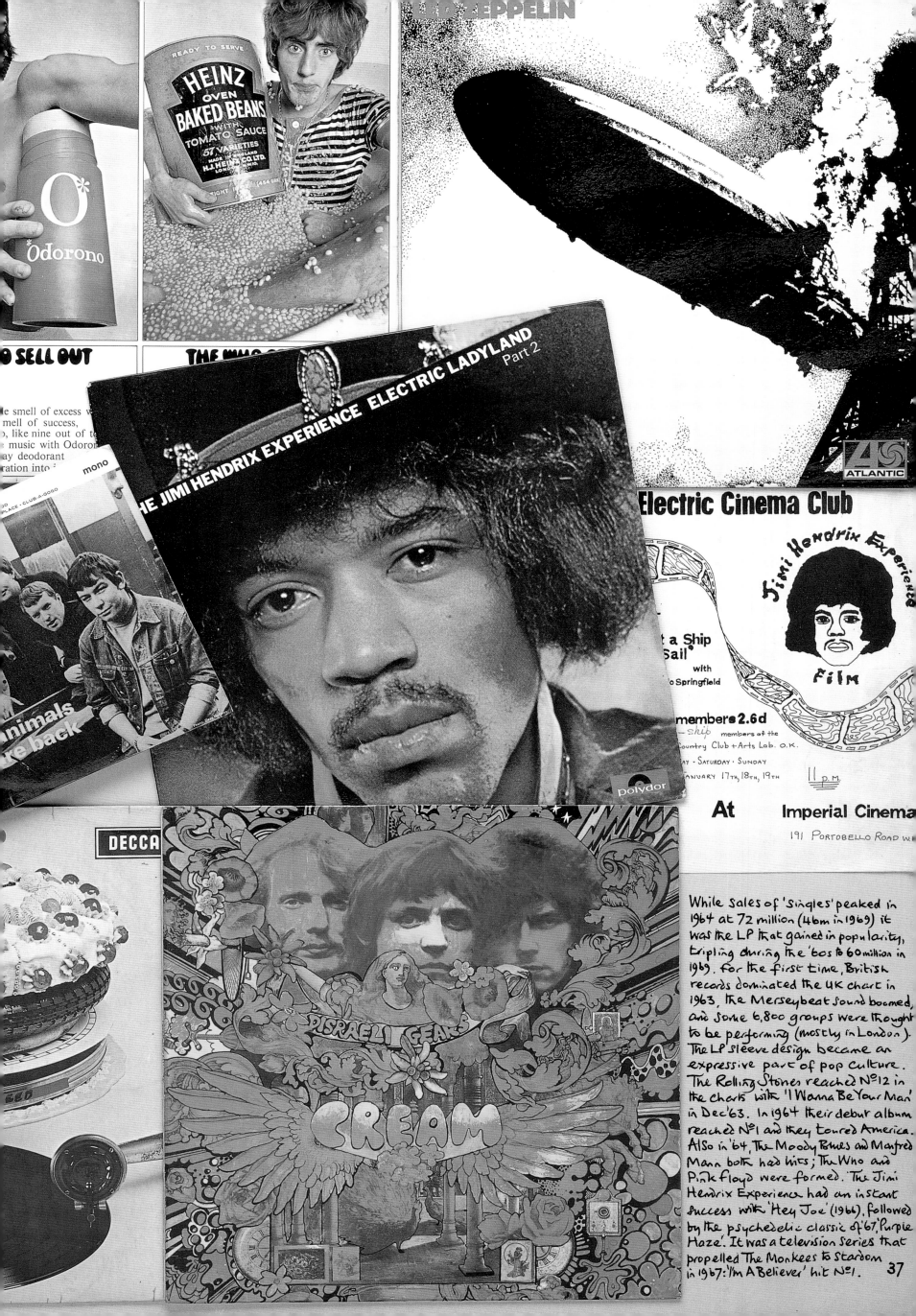

LED ZEPPELIN

ATLANTIC

HEINZ OVEN BAKED BEANS WITH TOMATO SAUCE 57 VARIETIES

Odorono

THE WHO

O SELL OUT

e smell of excess w
mell of success,
o, like nine out of te
music with Odoron
ay deodorant
ration into

mono

PLACE • CLUB-A-GOGO

animals
re back

THE JIMI HENDRIX EXPERIENCE   ELECTRIC LADYLAND   Part 2

Polydor

Electric Cinema Club

Jimi Hendrix Experience

Film

t a Ship
Sail
with
o Springfield

members 2.6d

—ship members of the
Country Club + Arts Lab. O.K.
y • Saturday • Sunday
ANUARY 17th, 18th, 19th   11 p.m.

At   Imperial Cinema

191 PORTOBELLO ROAD W

DECCA

DISRAELI GEARS

CREAM

While sales of 'singles' peaked in
1964 at 72 million (46m in 1969) it
was the LP that gained in popularity,
tripling during the '60s to 60 million in
1969. For the first time, British
records dominated the UK chart in
1963, the Merseybeat sound boomed,
and some 6,800 groups were thought
to be performing (mostly in London).
The LP sleeve design became an
expressive part of pop culture.
The Rolling Stones reached Nº12 in
the charts with 'I Wanna Be Your Man'
in Dec '63. In 1964 their debut album
reached Nº1 and they toured America.
Also in '64, The Moody Blues and Manfred
Mann both had hits; The Who and
Pink Floyd were formed. The Jimi
Hendrix Experience had an instant
success with 'Hey Joe' (1966), followed
by the psychedelic classic of '67, 'Purple
Haze'. It was a television series that
propelled The Monkees to stardom
in 1967: 'I'm A Believer' hit Nº1.

37

JOIN YOUR FRIENDS AT THE ROVER'S RETURN

CORONATION STREET

SET OF SIX GLASSES

ENA SHARPLES
ALBERT TATLOCK
ANNIE WALKER

MARTHA LONGHURST
JACK WALKER
MINNIE CALDWELL

PATRICIA PHOENIX • VIOLET CARSON
CORONATION STREET

GRANADA TELEVISION'S
CORONATION STREET
Jigsaw SIZE 17"x11"

GRANADA TV'S
CORONATION STREET
JIGSAW 340 PIECES Approx. Size 17"x11"

4. ENA AT BAY

ROYAL COURT THEATRE LIVERPOOL
Proprietors: Howard and Wyndham Ltd. Managing Director: Stewart Cruikshank Telephone: Roya
Manager: Josep
FOR ONE WEEK commencing MONDAY, 7th SEPTEMB
EVENINGS (Monday to Friday) at 7.30 SATURDAY (Two perf.) at 5 &
PRICES OF ADMISSION: Boxes 36/- Stalls: 10/6, 8/6 Grand Circle: 10/6, 9/- Back Stalls: 5/6 Balcony/
rus Presentations in association with James Whitley Limited

CORONATION STREET
TELEVISION STARS

N BEAVIS LYNNE CAROL DOREEN KEOGH FRANK PEMBER

irm foundatio
rip roaring farce by 'Coronation Street' writers
rected by JAMES BELCHAMBER
JOHN F
VINCE PO

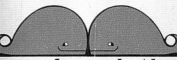

The first transistor radio had been made in the USA in 1954 (in Britain from 1956). Convenient to hold or put in the shirt pocket, the transistor became a popular accessory, like those shown opposite from the late 1950s and the 1960s. The first imported transistor from Japan was the Sony TR620 (top left corner), measuring 2¼" x 3½"; it cost £18.18.0, first arriving in Britain during 1960. Granada's Coronation Street was first televised in December 1960 (being nationally networked after 6 months); by 1965 it was Britain's most popular TV show. 39

HERE'S HARRY

PEGGY MOUNT DAVID KOSSOFF

THE LARKINS
Saturday 8.10 p.m.

Richard Briers and Prunella Scales in
The Marriage Lines
A new TV comedy series
SEE PAGE 41

ANOTHER RADIO TIMES COMPETITION
FIT-A-FEATUR
£2,000 IN PRIZES: See page 28

MAY 1

Radio Times (Incorporating World Radio) May 10, 1962. Vol. 155: No. 2069.

BBC
Radio Times
tv and SOUND

THE Rag Trade
FRIDAY TV

Radio Times (Incorporating World-Radio) November 28, 1963. Vol. 161. No. 2010.

NOVEMBER 3

Radio Times
SIXPENCE   NORTH OF ENGLAND EDITION

COMPACT celebrates
SEE PAGE 27

MIDLAND EDITION   No 411   SEPTEMBER 13, 1963   6ᵈ

TV TIM

CHARLIE DRAKE
starts his life story inside

Radio Times (Incorporating World Radio) July 11, 1963. Vol. 160. No. 2070.

JULY 13—19

BBC
Radio Times   tv
FIVEPENCE   SOUTH AND WEST EDITION   Sound

Dick Emery's
SATURDAY TV SHOW
in which he is joined by
Joan Sims
SEE PAGE 7

RADIO TIMES COMPETITION
FIT-A-FEATURE
£2,000 IN PRIZES: See page 18

Radio Times (Incorporating World-Radio) September 26, 1963. Vol. 160. No. 2081.

Radio Tim
SIXPENCE   SOUTH AN

tw twtw

LONDON EDITION   No 414   OCTOBER 4, 1963   6ᵈ   OCT 6 to

TV TIMES

S
ROGER M
Jackie
Sunday 7.28

The satirical programme 'That Was The Week That Was' attacked the establishment and in particular the government. Opening in Nov 1962, it was taken off air by the BBC in Dec 1963 before the coming 1964 general election.

40

KEITH BARRON
AS
LUCKY JIM

WELCOME TO
ARDEN HOUSE

...BUT ALSO

FEBRUARY 27—

Radio Times

NORTHERN IRELAND EDITION

Midlands and E. Anglia April 12-18

Radio Times EIGHTPE BBC t

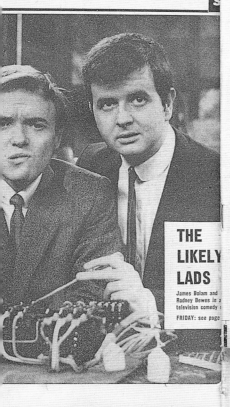

THE
LIKELY
LADS

James Bolam and
Rodney Bewes in a
television comedy
FRIDAY: see page

Radio Times October 19, 1967
LONDON AND SOUTH-EAST

Radio Times BBC

OCTOBER

EIGH

simon
DUDUDUD
Deetime

EVERY SATURDAY ON

Simon and
family—
week's Sta

DEREK
NIMMO
AND
FELIX
AYLMER
in *Oh Brother!*
BBC1

Midlands and E. Anglia JANUARY 18-24

Radio Times EIGHTPE BBC t

THE
TROUBLESHOOTERS
EVERY MONDAY ON BBC

An interview with Bob Arnold (Tom Forrest) of The Archers SEE PAGE

JUNE 1

BBC

Radio Times

LONDON AND SOUTH-EAST

BBC

ADAM
ADAMANT
LIVES!

ROLF
HARRIS
BBC.1
SATURDAY

In 1960 half the population watched
television; by the end of the '60s
most, who wanted one, had a TV set.
Comedy and drama made many actors
household names. Harry Worth, Charlie
Drake, Morecambe and Wise all featured throughout the decade, while The Dick
Emery Show ran from 1963. Both Dr. Finlay's Casebook and Steptoe & Son began
in 1962. The highlights of 1960s television included The Larkins (1958-64), The
Rag Trade (1961-3), Compact (1962-5), The Saint (1962-9), Marriage Lines (1963-6),
Not Only...But Also (1964-5), The Likely Lads (1964-6), Adam Adamant Lives (1966-9),
Lucky Jim (from 1966), Till Death Us Do Part (from 1966) Oh Brother! (from 1968) and
Dad's Army (from 1968). New for '69 were Monty Python's Flying Circus, and a sci-fi prog, Star Trek.

As people watched more television, so cinema audiences dropped; by 1967 there were just 1,800 cinemas in the UK (4,500 in 1950). Epics like 'Cleopatra' (1963) helped to steady the decline, and films based on TV hits tried to boost audiences with Morecambe & Wise's 'The Intelligence Men' (1966), 'Thunderbirds' (1966) and 'Till Death Us Do Part' (1969). Films ranged from the kitchen sink drama of 'Saturday Night and Sunday Morning' (1960) to the musical 'The Sound of Music' (1965). American success included 'Bonnie & Clyde' (1967), 'The Graduate' (1967) and Clint Eastwood's spaghetti westerns. 43

By 1960 the novels by Ian Fleming on the exploits of Agent 007, James Bond, had become worldwide best sellers. The films that followed were equally successful, even though the first, Dr. No, was only allocated the conservative budget of $1 million by United Artists. Dr. No, starring Sean Connery as Bond and Ursula Andress as Honey Ryder, was released in 1962 and quickly exceeded expectations. There followed: From Russia With Love (1963), Goldfinger (1964), Thunderball (1965) now with a $5.6m budget, and You Only Live Twice (1967). On Her Majesty's Secret Service (1969) was released with George Lazenby as Bond. Fleming's first novel Casino Royale (1953) was made into a satirical film in 1967 with Peter Sellers as Bond.

44

Exciting
AUSTIN mini

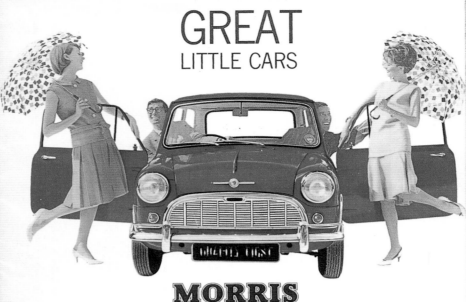

GREAT LITTLE CARS

MORRIS
MINI-MINORS

New HI

Austin Healey
SPRITE MK II

MK II

FORD OF BRITAIN □ CONSUL
Cortina

EWC 935

The new 1961
VAUXHALLS
Victor
Velox
Cresta

built for the Motorway age

HE JAGUAR "E" TYPE G.T. OPEN TWO-SEATER

CORGI
PRECISION DIE-CAS

DINKY TOYS

Boys learnt about cars through playing with Dinky, Corgi or Matchbox toys.

"MATCHBOX" COLLECTORS CATALOGUE

MY PICTURE BOOK OF
MOTORS

A NURSERY COLOUR PICTURE BOOK

A
lifetime
of safe
motoring
ahead !

Learn to drive with the...

BRITISH
SCHOOL
OF
MOTORING

L

A new freedom for motoring came with the opening of motorways. At the end of 1959, 73 miles of the M1 were built; by 1967 there were 500 miles of motorway driving. In 1960 there were 5.5 million cars, by the end of the decade there were twice that number. Small cars like the Mini (launched in 1959) made motoring more affordable, and sales accelerated when the Mini Cooper won the Monte Carlo Rally of 1964. The alluring lines of the E-type Jaguar arrived in 1961, Consul Cortina (1963), Ford Escort (1968) and Ford Capri (1969).

46

It was Wonderful!

Come Abroad with Us

says Hughie Green & Deidre

Silverline TOURS

CONTINENTAL

TORREMOLINOS

15 Days of Sun and Beach, Antiquity and Beauty.
Golf and Tennis, Gastronomy and Imbibing . . . .
from 61 guineas inclusive of air fare, hotel, with

Horizon

MAJORCA

SHOWING THE RESORTS IN WHICH CONTINENTAL VILLAS
HAVE LEASED THEIR PROPERTIES FOR 1962.

SUNTOURS

SUNSHINE AIR HOLIDAYS 1962

VILLAS FLATS CHALETS SPAIN

BRITISH UNITED AIRWAYS

JERSEY and G

SKY HO

HORIZON TRAVEL

Duty-free import con

VILLAS ABROAD

SUMMER 1962

B·O·A·C BAR SERVICE

SkyTours

Queen Elizabeth 2

CUNARD

With increasingly economical flights provided by aeroplanes like the Boeing 707-436 (from 1960), Trident (1964), BAC Super VC10 (1965) and BAC One-Eleven (1968), the cost of travel became more affordable. Package holidays boomed in the sun of Greece, Italy and especially Spain with exotic destinations like Majorca, Ibiza, Tossa de Mar and Torremolinos, "the carefree atmosphere will appeal to the most discerning holiday-maker acquiring a deep tan on the fine sandy beach". In Britain, the services of British Rail encouraged travel with rover tickets and bargain breaks, although Beeching's axe closed 3,800 miles of track between 1963 and 1967. The Hovercraft began to carry passengers in 1962, and a cross-Channel service in '68.

THE ITALIAN BEACHES

AIR HOLIDAYS ABROAD 1962

FROM TRIESTE TO REGGIO CALABRIA AND SICILY

48

No.1 OF A NEW PAPER WITH A LOVELY *Gift*

Princess

Sunshine Weekly

A FIVE STAR WEEKLY **FREE** in №1 OF A SMA... NEW P...

BUSTER

Son of Andy Capp

Bimbo

PRICE 5D

FREE INSIDE! *FLYING MODEL* of the T.S.R.2.

Hurricane

29th FEBRUARY, 1964 — EVERY MONDAY 6d

ANOTHER GREAT FREE GIFT FOR YOU INSIDE!

WHAM!

No. 3 4 JULY 1964 EVERY TUESDAY 6d.

No. 1—JANUARY 23, 1965. PRICE 5d.

Sparky

FREE! in this issue...an exciting B

T TORN

No.1 JANUARY 14, 1967

FEATURING ALL-ACTION: BATMAN · VOYAGE TO THE
BONANZA · UNCLE · SUPERMAN · TARZAN · PHAN...

Batman &

Tarzan

The Man from U.N.C.L.E

FREE in №1 OF A NEW PAPER FOR GIRLS
A LOVELY FLORAL BRACELET

Sunshine Weekly

June

© Fleetway Publications Ltd. 1961.

4½ 18th March, 1961

EVERY TUESDAY

11 SEPT 1965 VOL. I. No. 1

WOMAN'S REALM

Story Time
for little children

© Odhams Press Ltd · England 1965

EVERY TUESDAY 7d

No.1—JAN. 21, 1967

Man...

EVERY THURSDAY

A very Happy Christmas to all our readers !

Yogi Bear's Own
Hanna-Barbera

HAPPY CHRISTMAS

Weekly

Week ending December 22, 1962

6d

FREE WI...

№1 **FREE** *JET SCREAMER* INSIDE!

Champion

26th FEBRUARY, 1966 EVERY MONDAY 7d

IT ZOOMS
IT SOARS
IT DIVES
IT ROARS

Here is
super
for
It is
this
Sto...

With Gerry Anderso...

TV C...

No. 17 UNIVERSE EDITION

**FIREBA...
FLIGHT...**

XL5

FREE INSIDE! GIANT WALL PICTURE OF HUCK AND YOGI!

Extra big issue of . . .

HUCKLEBERRY HOUND
Hanna-Barbera

6

Weekly

NOW THAT I'VE BOUGHT A PROFESSIONAL-TYPE CAMERA, I'LL GET A JOB AS A NEWS PHOTOGRAPHER!

DAILY SNOOZE

Week ending November 24, 1962

★ **FREE** INSIDE! THE GUN WITH THE **BIG** BANG! ★

SMASH!

No.1 5th. FEB. 1966 EVERY THURSDAY

STOP SHAKING AND SELL US SOME COPIES, TOO! WITH THOSE BANGING GUNS WE'LL SCARE OFF EVERY CROOK IN TOWN !

GET YOUR FREE GIFT GUN IN HERE

FREE WITH SMASH!

SMASH! OUT

NEWSAGENT

SQUIRT!

No.1 of a wonderful new paper with an exciting GIFT

TV Toyland

28th MAY 1966 EVERY MONDAY 7D

THE B-I-G NEW PAPER FOR BOYS

Boys' World

26 January 1963 Vol. I No. 1 EVERY MONDAY 6d.

FREE INSIDE

NO. 1 OF THE NEW COLOURED PICTURE WEEKLY FOR THE VERY YOUNG VIEWER
FREE INSIDE . . . A PUNCH GLOVE PUPPET

PIPPIN 7D

Every Monday · Week Ending 24th September, 1966 · Number One

FREE Inside!
lovely stand-up figures of
PINKY and PERKY

THIS SUPER
PATHFINDER
COMPASS

The free gift was still an essential part of selling-in a new comic — cardboard guns were especially popular. Dramatic titles were favoured: Wham! (1964), Smash (1966), Jag (1968), Pow! (1967); while for girls it was names like June (1961), Mandy (1967) or Sally (1969). But television was the great influence: Huckleberry Hound (1961), Yogi Bear (1962), TV Toyland (1966) and Pippin (1966), named after the character in the children's TV series Pogles Wood (1964) created by the same team as The Clangers (1969). In 1965 TV Century 21 was published in full-colour photogravure with a dateline of 2065, 100 years ahead; the contents were mostly devoted to Gerry Anderson's TV heroes (he licensed the comic).

No. 1 WITH FREE GIFT INSIDE
BOBBY MOORE'S BOOK of the F.A. CUP
JAG 7D
4th MAY 1968

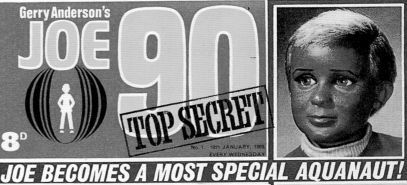

Gerry Anderson's
JOE 90
8D TOP SECRET
No.1. 18th JANUARY, 1969
EVERY WEDNESDAY
JOE BECOMES A MOST SPECIAL AQUANAUT!

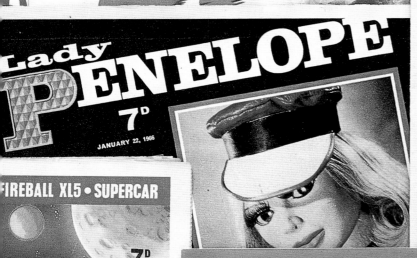

Lady PENELOPE 7D
JANUARY 22, 1966

FIREBALL XL5 • SUPERCAR
7D
...TURE IN the 21st CENTURY
DATELINE: May 15, 2065
MYSTERY
...LAMP-DOWN ON
...CITY SECURITY!

Sevenpence
TV COMIC
Free inside A KEN DODD mask!
Every Monday
Week Ending 3rd February, 1968
Number 842
Ken Dodd's DIDDYMEN

FREE GIFT INSIDE!
MAC'S JET CAR KIT!
IT REALLY WORKS!
JOIN...
WORLD INTELLIGENCE NETWORK
WIN
SUPER TV STRIPS

No. 1 of the new coloured picture weekly for the young viewer 7D
FREE INSIDE...a Sooty glove puppet!
Playland
Every Wednesday   Week Ending 13th January, 1968   Number One
Sooty and Sweep

Nº1 OF A LOVELY NEW PAPER
ALL IN COLOUR WITH A FREE GIFT 7D
22nd MARCH, 1969 EVERY MONDAY
Bobo Bunny

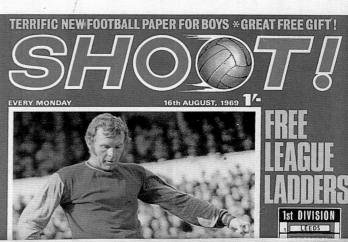

No1 OF A SUPER NEW GIRLS' PAPER
EVERY MONDAY 14th JUNE, 1969
6D
Sally

FREE IDENTIKIT INSIDE
The VALIANT IDENTIKIT WANTED
VALIANT
BRITAIN'S SUPER-HERO ACTION COMIC

NEW COMIC FOR THE NEW BREED OF COMIC FANS
POW! No.1 21st JAN 1967 EVERY MONDAY 7d
...EE INSIDE
THE WEB-CENTRE SPIDER-MATIC
FREE WITH POW! BRITAIN'S NEW FUN AND THRILLS PAPER!

FANTASTIC AND TERRIFIC
A POWER COMIC
No. 52   EVERY MONDAY   9d
FREE INSIDE!
STAR TARGET PISTOL
PLUS THOR...
Dr. STRANGE...
...THE X-MEN...
...And THE MIGHTY AVENGERS

TERRIFIC NEW FOOTBALL PAPER FOR BOYS * GREAT FREE GIFT!
SHOOT!
EVERY MONDAY   16th AUGUST, 1969   1/-
FREE LEAGUE LADDERS
1st DIVISION
LEEDS

LOOK, GIRLS AND BOYS! TWO COMICS FOR ONLY 6D
WHIZZER and CHIPS
EVERY MONDAY 25th OCTOBER, 1969
FREE GIFT INSIDE
SUPER CARTOON Flick Book
"CHIPS" IS INSIDE "WHIZZER"
SID'S SNAKE

52 Toys for the boys involved motoring — motorways, minis and the E-type Jag, t'Beat the Warden' (traffic wardens appeared in London 19

Action Man made his mark from 1966 (in the USA — was GI Joe, 1964), Twister from 1965 and TV games like Danger Man (1960-8), Spy Catcher (1959-60) and ITV's The Larkins (1958-64). The Spacehopper bounced along in 1968 (see page 1).

For the youngest viewers Watch With Mother continued to show many of the favourites from the 1950s – Andy Pandy, The Flowerpot Men and Rag, Tag & Bobtail. Then the creations of Hanna-Barbera took over: Huckleberry Hound (1959-64) with Yogi Bear and Mr Jinks the cat, both featuring in their own right, The Flintstones (1961-6), Deputy Dawg, The Jetsons and Boss Cat all arrived in 1963. Gordon Murray Puppets created the animation of Camberwick Green in 1966 with a string of characters like Windy Miller and Mr Tripp the milkman; then came Trumpton in 1967. Magic Roundabout first appeared in 1965 with Dylan the rabbit, Dougal the dog, Brian the snail, Ermintrude the cow, Zebedee the spring man and

so Florence, Mr MacHenry and Mr Rusty. Another French import was Hector's House in 1968.
a foxy Basil Brush had his own show from 1968. Ray Allan's ventriloquist act with Tich and Quackers began in 1966 (see p.60).
r older children there was no escape from Dr Who and the Daleks (1963) with William Hartnell playing Dr Who till 1966 and then
atrick Troughton till 1969. Z Cars began in 1962 and featured the Ford Zephyr patrol cars. The Man from UNCLE (1965-68)
arred Robert Vaughn and David McCallum — in 1967 it was Stephanie Powers as The Girl from UNCLE. More annuals
page 60 : Dr Kildare (1961-6) and The Avengers (1961-9) starring Patrick Macnee (John Steed), Honor Blackman (til'64) then Diana Rigg.

Having produced the television puppet series 'The Adventures of Twizzle' in 1956, Gerry Anderson went on to create more

56 puppet adventures in the 1960s: Supercar (1961); Fireball XL5 (1963) with Steve Zodiac, prof Matthew Matic, Zero

and Venus; Stingray (1964) with Troy Tempest; Thunderbirds (1965) with Jeff Tracy, Brains and the London agent Lady
Penelope who had a pink Rolls Royce FAB1; Captain Scarlet and the Mysterons (1967), and in 1968 the boy wonder Joe90. 57

Fact meets fiction — as the space race intensified, so the fictional ideas of the toy industry took on the factual realities of the moon probe story.

The Russian Lunik 2 had reached the moon in 1959. By 1961 man was in space; in 1964 pictures of the moon's surface came back from Ranger 7. Space walks began in 1965; orbits of the moon were achieved during 1966. Then on 21 July 1969 the lunar model of Apollo 11 put Neil Armstrong and Buzz Aldrin on the moon, returning to earth in their space capsule with astronaut Michael Collins. 100 million watched on TV.

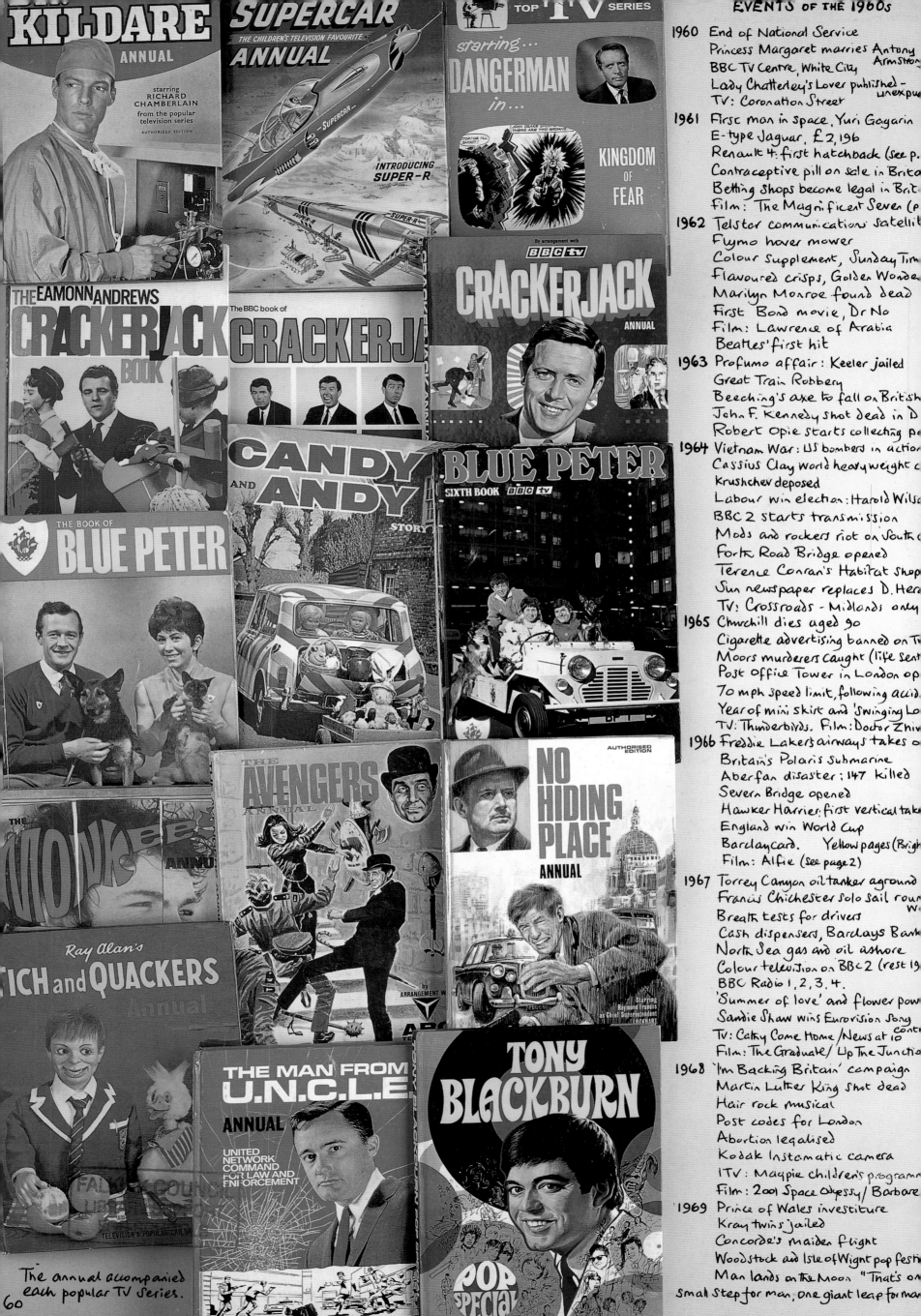

EVENTS OF THE 1960s

1960 End of National Service
Princess Margaret marries Antony Armstrong
BBC TV Centre, White City
Lady Chatterley's Lover published - unexpu
TV: Coronation Street

1961 First man in space, Yuri Gagarin
E-type Jaguar, £2,196
Renault 4: first hatchback (see p.
Contraceptive pill on sale in Brita
Betting shops become legal in Brit
Film: The Magnificent Seven (p

1962 Telstar communication satellit
Flymo hover mower
Colour supplement, Sunday Tim
Flavoured crisps, Golden Wonde
Marilyn Monroe found dead
First Bond movie, Dr No
Film: Lawrence of Arabia
Beatles' first hit

1963 Profumo affair: Keeler jailed
Great Train Robbery
Beeching's axe to fall on British
John F. Kennedy shot dead in D
Robert Opie starts collecting pa

1964 Vietnam War: US bombers in action
Cassius Clay world heavyweight c
Krushchev deposed
Labour win election: Harold Wilso
BBC 2 starts transmission
Mods and rockers riot on South c
Forth Road Bridge opened
Terence Conran's Habitat shop
Sun newspaper replaces D. Hera
TV: Crossroads - Midlands only

1965 Churchill dies aged 90
Cigarette advertising banned on TV
Moors murderers caught (life sent
Post Office Tower in London op
70 mph speed limit, following accid
Year of mini skirt and 'Swinging Lo
TV: Thunderbirds. Film: Doctor Zhiv

1966 Freddie Laker's airways takes o
Britain's Polaris submarine
Aberfan disaster: 147 killed
Severn Bridge opened
Hawker Harrier: first vertical take
England win World Cup
Barclaycard.   Yellow pages (Brigh
Film: Alfie (see page 2)

1967 Torrey Canyon oil tanker aground
Francis Chichester solo sail roun W
Breath tests for drivers
Cash dispensers, Barclays Bank
North Sea gas and oil ashore
Colour television on BBC2 (rest 19
BBC Radio 1, 2, 3, 4.
'Summer of love' and flower pow
Sandie Shaw wins Eurovision Song
TV: Cathy Come Home/News at 10 cont
Film: The Graduate/ Up The Junctio

1968 'I'm Backing Britain' campaign
Martin Luther King shot dead
Hair rock musical
Post codes for London
Abortion legalised
Kodak Instamatic camera
ITV: Magpie children's programm
Film: 2001 Space Odyssey/ Barbare

1969 Prince of Wales investiture
Kray twins jailed
Concorde's maiden flight
Woodstock and Isle of Wight pop festi
Man lands on the Moon "That's on
small step for man, one giant leap for man

The annual accompanied each popular TV series.